New and Selected Poems

THE PALMETTO POETRY SERIES
NIKKY FINNEY, SERIES EDITOR

Ota Benga under My Mother's Roof
Carrie Allen McCray, edited by Kevin Simmonds

A Book of Exquisite Disasters
Charlene Monahan Spearen

Seeking: Poetry and Prose Inspired by the Art of Jonathan Green
Edited by Kwame Dawes and Marjory Wentworth

New and Selected Poems
Marjory Wentworth

New and Selected Poems

Marjory Wentworth

Foreword by Carol Ann Davis

The University of South Carolina Press

© 2014 University of South Carolina

Published by the University of South Carolina Press
Columbia, South Carolina 29208

www.sc.edu/uscpress

Manufactured in the United States of America

23 22 21 20 19 18 17 16 15 14   10 9 8 7 6 5 4 3 2 1

Library of Congress Cataloging-in-Publication Data

Wentworth, Marjory, 1958–
    [Poems. Selections]
    New and selected poems / Marjory Wentworth.
        pages cm. — (The Palmetto Poetry Series)
    ISBN 978-1-61117-322-2 (pbk. : alk. paper) —
    ISBN 978-1-61117-323-9 (ebook)
    1. Title.
    PS3623.E58A6 2014
    811'.6—dc23

                                    2013027969

This book was printed on a recycled paper with 30 percent postconsumer
waste content.

For my mother, Mary Kneeland Heath

Contents

.

Foreword

It is difficult
to get the news from poems
yet men die miserably every day
for lack
of what is found there.

> "Asphodel, That Greeny Flower,"
> *William Carlos Williams*

In poetry circles it has become *de riguer* to quote William Carlos Williams' famous lines, but how relevant his sentiment still is, given our common experience of so much "news" passing by us unexamined, reckoned with momentarily or not at all, and put away without any sense of how we may be implicated by it.* I like to think of Elizabeth Bishop's gentle "answer" to Williams, an elaboration, really, as she elegantly explodes assumptions we hold about the fixed nature of knowledge (an idea closely related to Williams' "news")—opening a vast ocean between certainty and doubt—in her unforgettable ending to "At the Fishhouses." Williams includes his warning

---

*Epigraph excerpted from "Asphodel, That Greeny Flower," by William Carlos Williams, from *The Collected Poems, Volume II, 1939–1962,* copyright © 1994 by William Carols Williams. Reprinted by permission of New Directions Publishing Corp.

about the threat represented by our commonly-lived yet unexamined life within the context of a long love poem—a praise poem at heart—a poem arguing for the redemptive possibility of knowledge-as-sensory experience, his famous words about news and dying miserably all in the service of the love of "Asphodel, that Greeny Flower." As with Williams' flower, Bishops' poem at first seems an unassuming description of the shore near the fishhouses of her childhood Nova Scotia. Yet this description becomes a complicated comparison between water and knowledge, hiding in its belly an important distinction. "It," the water, is

> like what we imagine knowledge to be:
> dark, salt, clear, moving, utterly free,
> drawn from the cold hard mouth
> of the world, derived from the rocky breasts
> forever, flowing and drawn, and since
> our knowledge is historical, flowing, and flown.*

Bishop reminds us here that hard-won "knowledge is historical," and because it is, it is always leaving us, "flowing and flown." It would be a mistake to believe history, therefore; instead, one must experience the watery world, and experience knowledge's flight. Her argument fits hand in glove with Williams' in that it requires the exploration of all that is "dark, salt, clear, moving, utterly free," and posits the witnessing of the thing (our experience) drawn "From the cold hard mouth/ of the world" as that which keeps not just the art of poetry, but "men"—if Williams is right—alive. It is the poet who must "derive" from "rocky breasts" this knowledge or risk dying from "lack of what is found there;" it is also the poet who must remind us "our knowledge is historical," and therefore a moving, a participatory sport. Vigilance is necessary. Reader and writer are implicated in a beautifully sensual, but politically urgent, mutual gaze.

It is from this tradition of the urgency of poetic exploration, the need to describe the world as she finds it, that Marjory Wentworth's accomplished *New and Selected Poems* springs. Like her literary forebears, Wentworth addresses simultaneously political realities and personal ones, showing again and again throughout her collection the urgent relationship between the two through the use of concrete images that implicate the speaker and draw her into questions about historical knowledge. Sometimes, even stones have violent histories, as when "one stone" is "rubbed smooth in an earthquake." It is through image that Marjory treats us to both the bitter and the sweet simultaneously, asking the reader, with her generous but persistently questioning intellect, to draw the finer and truer difficult conclusion. The stone may be smooth, but it has been through something to please our eye. Perhaps no pleasing thing is unharmed, the poem seems to suggest.

The persistence of Wentworth's inquiry is not immediately evident; early poems introduce major themes that develop and deepen in crucial ways during the progress of the collection. It is as if the early poems pose questions that the late poems answer, or warnings heard from a great distance in the early work are faced with all their threat and clarity in the later poems, which address issues such as human trafficking and genocide directly, and even blend such subjects with the experience of motherhood, as happens most acutely in the late poems "Manacles" and "In Gaza's Berry Fields." Motherhood haunts "A Monstrous Terrible Story," in which Wentworth chooses first to describe with Bishopian care the "stray dog" and "young fisherman" who find "the decomposing bodies of fifteen young girls" and "barrels" of "hundreds / of curled human fetuses" respectively. Such descriptive treatment of horrific events demands our attention, not just intellectually but somatically, because of Wentworth's devotion to the image. Here is the difficult obverse to Williams' imagistic praise song: the sense-laden elegy, the world-weary, detail-rich lament.

Wentworth never averts her gaze from the unthinkable, but accepts, too, the bounty offered by everyday grace. In fact, it is this service she provides to the reader, inserting us into the bind we all feel, bridging with her observational manner the distance between the richness of one's experience of the world and the fact of its unforgiving, even self-killing violence. Thank goodness, then, that winter is full of "faucets" that "drip all night," elegies occur inside a delicate "blue hour," and the "undertow" calls us to enter it. In fact, "Undertow" seems to announce the collection's strategy, becoming its ars poetica: it suggests that reading a poem is an only mildly dangerous, ordinary "tempting thing" that might ask us to "go somewhere unexpected." With such modest beginnings—it is just swimming, reader, just moving one's arms in the water of language—who expects to be drawn in and under?

Yet Wentworth manages just such an immersion. By giving us the ordinary world we recognize in so many images, Wentworth opens us up to "the news" that we don't (or won't) recognize as connected to tragedy until she places them in proximity. I pick berries with my children, though thankfully, I have not lost a child (much less seven!) in berry fields to planted mines, as the mother in Gaza did, but how terrifying—and yet how essential—to understand all we have in common. Williams is right. It is "difficult to get the news from poems." But it is not impossible, and it could not be more necessary. In such sure poetic hands, we are that one stone rubbed smooth in an earthquake, or we are its witness, the bird that flits overhead, resting "among sweet faces." What earthquakes have we been through to arrive here, smooth as a stone? Wentworth invites us to imagine for ourselves the mysteries and contradictions of our own experience, witness to all that is "flowing and flown" in ourselves as well as in the news. In a world that seems as fractured today as it must have to Williams in another "low, dishonest" century, Marjory Wentworth reminds us of the life-giving force of the witnessing intellect, deep, careful, heartfelt, and muscular. You are in good hands, reader. Enjoy the under-tow; may you "go somewhere unexpected."

CAROL ANN DAVIS

June 2013

Poems from Noticing Eden

In the Dream of the Sea

I call you from the open water
surrounding us, speaking
across divided lives.

I call you
from the waves
that always have direction.

Where strings of morning glory
hold the dunes in place,
I call. In winter,

when wind pours
through cracks in the walls.
Inside, I call

although my voice
has been silent
and dissolving.

In sand
pulled back
into the body

of the sea,
from the blue
house built on sand

balanced at the edge
of the world
I call you.

Drowning stars,
shipwrecks, and broken voices
move beneath the waves.

Here, at the open
center
of my ordinary heart

filling with sounds
of the resurrected,
in the dream

of the sea,
I call you
home.

Barrier Island

Where nothing is certain, we awaken
to another night of delicate rain
falling as if it didn't want to
disturb anyone. On and off
foghorns groan. The lighthouse beacon
circles the island. For hours, melancholy
waves tear whatever land we're standing on.
Listen to the sea—rain dripping
through fog, suspended at the edge of earth
on a circle of sand where we are always
moving slowly toward land.

Carolina Umbra

Boats fly out of the Atlantic
and moor themselves in my backyard
where tiny flowers, forgotten
by the wind, toss their astral heads
from side to side. Mouths ablaze, open,
and filling with rain.

After the hurricane, you can see
the snapped open drawbridge slide
beneath the waves on the evening news.
You go cold imagining
such enormous fingers of wind
that split a steel hinge until
its jaw opens toward heaven.

Above the twisted house,
above this island, where the torn
churches have no roofs, and houses
move themselves around the streets
as if they were made of paper;
tangled high in the oak branches,
my son's crib quilt waves its pastel flag.

But the crib rail is rusted shut.
And you can't see my children
huddled together on the one dry bed

of this home filling with birds
that nest in corners of windowless rooms,
or insects breeding in the damp sand
smeared like paint over the swollen floors.

The storm will not roar in your sleep
tonight, as if the unconscious
articulations of an animal aware
of the end of its life were trapped
in the many cages of your brain.

You can't see grief darken the wind
rising over the islands. Tonight,
as the burning mountains of debris
illuminate the sky for hundreds of miles,
I see only the objects of my life
dissolving in a path of smoke.

All the lost and scattered hours
are falling completely out of time.
where endless rows of shredded trees wait
with the patience of unburied
skeletons, accumulating in the shadows.

Wild Plums

I have walked this way before. Many times,
along these tangled paths to the sea,
I have seen the cardinals flashing
from the sweet myrtle, watched lizards
raise their heads to point the arrows
of their eyes. When I move my hands
through their world of wild beach flowers,
the yellow petals bleed a little at the center
each time they burst into flower.

Today there are hundreds of small plums descending
to the earth too soon. Like you, my friends,
they are wild, ripening, and fallen
to the ground which tears their skin
until it bleeds its thick sugary juice
across the sand. Flies are flocking.
But I can only gather handfuls of fruit
or flowers that were meant to die here,
and hold them for a little while.

The Nest of Stars

The night she died
stars were nesting
near my window.
The wind was so still
that echoes of the sea
were the only sounds
rising from the earth
until the howl
of one human heart
filled the universe.

Beach Walk

A man who looks like someone I once loved, passes me
on the beach today. The man is with a woman, of course.
This man I loved loves women, not in a lascivious way. He
    just
loves them. And he'd say it, just like that, *I love women, you*
    know.
Always have. She's a tall redhead, pulling a Black Lab
on a purple leash. Everyone on the beach wears shorts or
    T-shirts
and a bathing suit. The redhead has on heels. Her shirt is
    black.
Her pants are black. Odd choice of clothes for such a hot day.
    Mysterious,
now I think, symbolic. The man wears dark green sweat pants
and a gray sweat shirt. The clothes are hanging off of him
in big handfuls of soft cotton. Clothes like that must feel like
    pajamas.
From a distance, I don't notice his missing hair or the stillness
surrounding his diminished body that seems to glide over the
    sand
in slow motion. His hands in quiet fists at his sides. All of his
    energy
focused on moving his feet—one foot in front of the other
    foot.
His eyes look beyond the woman and the dog, toward the sea
glittering for miles in the sunlight. He is radiant

as he takes his last walk on the beach. Although exhaustion
and pain visibly press down on him like the inescapable heat,
he is completely happy to do this one thing. The only thing
   he's wanted
to do for months now, imagining every detail over and over
   again
in his hospital bed. This man who looks like someone
I once loved, looks like a man who is making love—
a man who is here, but not here.

Lament

If only you could touch my heart,
lie down and listen to the sad train
that passes through its center
and doesn't stop.

If only you could see
the way my heart is shifting
on the body's sands
like a moon shell
like a wooden box with black letters
like a castle
or a lost wheel
like a slashed and stranded sea turtle
tugging against the flood tide.

If only you could put your hand
into the mouth of the heart's wind
at night
into the mouth
of the loud wind
that wakes us
weeping.

If only you could help me
find the place
the wind is made.

Bring a blanket,
wine, forgiveness.

If we could gather
the bleached and broken bones
of the fish that escaped the net,
if we could scrub the bones clean
and plant them
like a garden
like a grave.

If we could only wash
away the blood
and drown the ghosts.

Toward the Sea

The wind is an empty place. You enter
expecting something softened by the sea.
A piece of cedar shaped into a body
you once loved. Perhaps the hand that held you
from a distance or the face that simply
held you here. Still moving in and out of time
during the hour when night meets day,
you try to find your bearings.
You pick up objects. You want to remember.
Jagged edged rocks in the palm of your hand.
You hold them up in the moonlight.
They are earthbound, filling with sky.
You walk on further, pause to scoop tiny iridescent
shells, the colors of cream and roses.
Little by little the air brightens into hours,
which are either empty or full of all the things
you love and remember, depending
on which direction the wind is coming from.

Hurricane Season

The blood moon thirsts. All night,
listening to unspoken prayers,
she tugs the sea beyond itself
until redundant waves retreating
wash the yellowed marshes clean.

In the heat that follows too much rain,
people crowd the churches.
On this September Sunday morning
their hymns begin to rise
and slap the winds still raging.

This is the music of bones
entwined in mortal language—

words of those who know the wind
erases every footprint carved in earth
where water, tired as a dreamer,
circling beneath oblivious clouds
blurs the variations painted on each human face.

Into the open womb of the sea
descend the ashes of our sins.

What keeps us here? Not gravity
or light, but rust on fences, holding
every house of swollen wood, an ache
a tooth, the day moon adrift
grinding tiny islands down to bone.

How the Yellow Angels Hunger

There was a time when the sky
could still crack open
releasing a daily sweep of birds
and light. There was a time
before the child left the world
in a blaze of color. It was
another universe, when
a pet parrot could sit
on a windowsill all night and gaze
at crowds of clinging angels
unravel in a gauze across the sky.

If only tears were silent
feathers. If only tears could be
simply made of salt and water
or rain, creeping down the windows
of this house where death screams
from corners of every room,
forcing its breath against panes of glass
until they shatter. For the living,
there is nothing but rain—
drops hammering the rooftop
like a flock of angry birds.

Above the wounded
house, where spirits gather
to chew on clouds
and weep for all of us,
there are angels.
Hidden hungry angels
with jaundiced halos
and angry fists
churning the air.

In their hands, bloom
bouquets of bloody feathers.
Little bandages of leaves
are sticking in the wind
as the building leans
its split shoulder
toward the outstretched
branches of a live oak,
which are always
reaching toward heaven.

As lamplight devours the one room
of this house, where time is
sitting still in a yellow chair
that will always be empty,
the blinded bird in the window
repeats, "Goodnight moon, good-
night moon, in the great green
room, in the great green."

The world will not stop
to see this room where a smile
is spreading on the face
of the man in the moon,
stitched into halves of satin sand

dollars and stars, swimming
on a blue crib quilt
that remembers laughter—
a crush of sand in a fist of fabric.

Now the birds are mute and hidden.
Their feathers float fluorescent
like sparks on the horizon.
But the clouds will not catch fire,
though the house is glowing
like a pumpkin with too many holes
carved in its body—that let in the rain,
dawn, and the chaos of birds.

Core Banks, North Carolina

Once whalers built their camps
atop tenuous fans of overwash,

now fishermen's junked cars
grow into drift and dune.

Infinity lives
in the damp bones of

abandoned things,
buried in the sand.

There is no stillness
in the sea spilling

into prehistoric inlets
carved into the sound.

An orange arc of moon sinks
in the middle of the sky .

Now there is wind,
the resurrection of water,

starlight
drowning in the tidal delta.

Findhorn

The sight of the ocean
always brings me home.
My childhood was one long day
with the sea. I even believed
that souls of the dead
swam beneath the water
until it touched an edge of the sky
and became heaven.

At low tide this beach is endless,
as flat and clear as the glass
pools of water collecting
between the dunes and the waves.
A pale moon rises. At midnight
little white lights begin to shine
on the offshore oil rig.
It is surreal. They say
this place is spiritual, mystical.
People in the community grow
giant cauliflower in the fertile soil.
I know nothing of the soil
and the fantastic vegetables,

but I do know
that I have never felt
closer to the dead.

I think of my father continuously
as I stare into the pink light
at the edge of the sea
where the sky is opening
to the setting sun.

The Color of Rain

Blue is the color of rain
falling in the night,
and brown is the river
that swallows rain.
Where the sun is
drowning in green
tea tinted water,
there are colors
giving birth in the rain.

River

The river is a woman who is never idle.
Into her feathering water
fall petals and bones

of earth's shed skins.
While all around her edges
men are carving altars,

the river gathers flotsam,
branches of time, and clouds
loosening the robes of their reflections.

Her dress is decoupage -
yellow clustering leaves,
ashes, paper, tin, and dung.

Wine dark honey for the world,
sweet blood of seeping magma
pulsing above the carbon starred

sediment. Striped with settled skulls,
wing, and leaf spine: the river
is an open-minded graveyard.

Listen to the music
of sunlight spreading
inside her crystal cells.

Magnet, clock, cradle
for the wind, the river holds a cup
filling with miles of rain.

But when the river sleeps,
her celestial children
break the sticks of gravity,

grab fistfuls of fish
scented amber clotted with diamonds,
ferns, and petalling clouds;

adorn bracelets of woven rain,
rise with islands of sweet grass
and stars strung to their backs

to wander over the scarred surface
of the earth, like their mothers
simply searching for the sea.

Irises

Irises bloom despite themselves,
acquiring beauty from the inherent
contradictions, like tulips turned
inside out and flaring into the bright
colors of a bruise. But sharp
green sworded ensiform will soon outgrow
and outnumber the crumbling flowers
risen from a stem, transformed
into leaves that pierce the night
breaking like fate above
the frail heads of irises.

Bamboo

Walking beside the cane break,
she watches small bright birds
weaving through the bamboo.
They glow at the edge of darkness,
like Christmas lights strung
in the mouth of a cave.

Behind the path, water
pours from a fountain
into a pool. The sound
is delicate, like rain
or distant bells.

Bamboo is elegant
and grows deliberately,
each section joined to the next
by a symmetrical scar.
Between them, the hollow stems
are filled with light.

The stems are tough and difficult
to break like her heart, rinsed clean.
Bamboo rises from the hillsides
a cathedral of calm green.
It has taken years for her
to find this place.

The Unkempt Garden

To find love
you must stumble many times
through its unkempt garden,
until roses growing wild along a fence
unfold and offer themselves to the wind.

Tear at the flowers with your teeth.
Let the sharp-tongued thorns
fill your mouth with kisses.
And petals, thick as rain, will slide
their offerings into you.

Homecoming

If sleep has a smell, it grows here
when flowers raise their heads in the mist
to eat the light pulsing at the edge of the sky
where tapered tails of wind unwind
like roots stumbling through darkness.

After the green silence of dreams
I rise and drink the warm rain falling,
dig two holes in the ground
to plant my tired feet,
because I need to live for awhile

in the black bed of earth. On this island
rolling beneath unfurled tongues of fog,
where the scent of wet salt can turn the air
to bread in my mouth, or blanch
the dark fisted vines that never wither.

All winter, jessamine and honeysuckle
holding petals in their closed mouths,
were waiting for desire
to open them, in the wind,
to lose themselves in rain.

When he is gone my heart rearranges
within my body, where nothing seems
to move for weeks or months. Alone
I wait for his scent to return
to the empty pillow beside me.

I am like the morning glory
embedded on our fence slats,
collapsing her purple flowers
that will resurrect and inflate
with mouthfuls of air.

The smell of grass releasing
after hours of warm rain
enters the open windows of our house.
Odors move from room to room like music.
My husband listens in his sleep.

On a couch in the living room, he listens.
With children curling like kittens around his feet,
he sleeps. Beneath pages of the Sunday paper,
cradled by all that is familiar, he sleeps.
Knowing the color of love, he sleeps.

The Coming Light

The wedding procession passes through the shadows
of an old oak growing between a graveyard and a church.
All day the sun burned through its branches. Flowers shriveled
on the headstones. Little flags hung limp on black sticks.

Now it is evening, and a wind moves off the sea.
It is a wind filled with tenderness, moving
across the bride's face like his breath, in the night
when he is kissing her. Sometimes,
when she looks at him while he is looking into her
it feels as if she is staring at the sun,
and she has to turn away. But it is too late.
She is already a woman in flames. She has forgotten
what life feels like without love. No ache and no hunger.

They have waited for twilight: to marry
in the copper colored air that feels like water
all around and holds them up like water does.

At the doorway, she isn't thinking about the veil
slipping off her head, or whether
her grandfather's wheelchair made it over the steps.
She sees the groom waiting at the end of a tunnel of light.

At the altar, he is turned away from her. A thin crucifix
lies flat against the beige cracked stone wall.
She is certain, that before everything and everyone
there was God, filling the air
where she walks into the coming light.

Near the Doorway

There may have been
An empty road, opening
Its hands for me.

Standing in the center of a field,
I watched fog spreading over the island
As layers of clouds streamed
Overhead. Birds in the trees
Were calling out to one another.

I couldn't tell their voices apart.
I couldn't see which branches they were calling from.

Looking down, I dreamed the earth
Was one field emptied of fog,

One house near the sea.

I began to walk.
Dark fires burned along the shore road.

Four flames
Four directions
Salt tossed in the wind.

Rain fell at my feet
Snow fell, far off.
Stone, star, cold, fire.

The birds suddenly silent
In the trees. I saw my voice.

Poems from Despite Gravity

Tangled

We return to hear the waves returning
to the beach, one after the other, connecting

us like blood. Long before we came
here, we were listening, remembering

wind, spinning salt, uninterrupted
sunlight. This is a place where dreams

return, fish bones tangled in seaweed.
Rinsed clean and kept, whatever sorrows

come are folded into the sea's
unbearable secrets.

Linthong

We are the foam
floating on a vast ocean.
We are the dust
wandering in endless space.
Our cries are lost
in the howling wind.

                    Unknown Vietnamese Refugee

I

Waiting in the JFK IMMIGRATION LINE
Linthong drinks from a metal fountain.
Water circles in the back of his throat.

He opens his plastic bag for inspection:
one comb, a pair of Levis, and a knife.

II

Swimming across
the Mekong River
open knife clenched
between his teeth
rope twisted
around the waist
of his sister
beside him

pulled under
ducking beneath
the moonlight
he dragged her
to a fishing boat
in the South China Sea
For weeks
they sailed with rice sacks
rigged to the mast
until a typhoon whipped
the cracked cotton to shreds
and pulled his sister
into the eager water when the winds died
they burned planks
torn from the deck
boiled sea water to
catch steam in a tube
drops on the tongue

III

In the Filipino camp,
ribs lined up
on his chest like a xylophone,
he learned English in the morning
and sold black market cigarettes
in the afternoon. Before he could sleep
he said the words *milk* and *highway,*
because he liked the sound.
He dreamed of California,
but he lives in Salem, Massachusetts,
in two rooms with eleven other people.
Every morning he goes to school
while the Lao fishermen take buses
to Gloucester to pack
fish into ice at the Gorton's Factory.
And the women stay behind

storing light bulbs, batteries,
and sneakers in the refrigerator,
leaving cooked rice and milk
in uncovered bowls on the cupboard.

IV

On Sundays Linthong chases sandpipers
in and out of the tide, pulsing
along the length of Singing Beach.
Dozens of spinnakers dot the horizon
like strange beautiful balloons.

He sits on a barnacled log,
tugs seaweed loose and chews.
Sucking on drops of ocean,
he watches fishermen
cast clear lines to the sea.

Sand

> The eye is not satisfied with seeing, not the ear
> with hearing.
>
> *Ecclesiastes*

Each day I awaken in darkness,
to the joy of that particular silence
when the earth becomes herself again
shedding centuries of clutter. Even here
the fort and cannons disappear. Every building
is erased by night. Only the moon and stars
remain and the waves rolling over sand
sounding like steady distant breaths.

Your breath is everywhere, dissolving like hours.
Only now can you enter my heart.
It is a small crowded place—
like this island, once a brief cluster
of weeds and sand, now filling
with high houses built one on top
of the other. Each one bigger than the last,
assuming a kind of permanence.

You have watched it all come and go.
Conquerors, pirates, soldiers and slaves.
Long battles at sea. The violence

that began a nation, and later divided it.
Consider the soldiers who washed up
like dead fish, or the countless Africans
who came ashore in chains and never left
the *lazaretto*. Buried in mass graves
unmarked and unvisited, they remain
and outnumber all who have followed.

Day after day the wind sweeps across the island
smothering the shattered bones and blood
in layers of swirling sand. I gather handfuls
and watch it scatter through my fingers.
This is all that remains
beneath the seaweed, stars and sweet myrtle;
sea birds scattered in the rain.

I lower my head and remember
this is where you live and suffer.
In the stillness I see the things that are
not visible. I hear voices
no one else can hear, except for you.

Strip Search

Survival is a form
of resistance. He knows
it will depend on small things,
like the sound of rodents

as they move
through the prison walls,
breaking the gray silence
falling everywhere in his cell.

He pulls down his pants
and turns around. Slowly
cotton falls around his ankles
like running water. The grass

growing through cracks in the floor
begins to flow beneath his feet,
as he waits for hands
and whatever they might hold

the animals are watching
like angels.

Dancing Barefoot in Atlanta

Tonight, for many reasons, I think
of my friend from Buenos Aires
who survived such horrific torture
that even now after all these years
I cannot write about it,
although he told me everything.

I remember his lost shoes
at a crowded party
where we danced for hours
only with each other.

I think of his soft scarred hands,
his voice quietly speaking into my ear,
his small body holding onto me.

And though we never fell in love
and he was old enough to be my father
when I think about my life's
most extraordinary moments
I am dancing, barefoot
in Atlanta Georgia
in the arms of the bravest man
I will ever know.
And he is laughing.

The Last Night

Drinking pints of lager and lime
like any other night, we talk
until the cigarette butts overflow
spreading ashes in the darkness.
Beneath the table, your prayer
beads click as unconsciously
as the chiming church bells.
The beads shine in your palm
like little black eyes. Five pairs

stare from the family photograph
taped above your cot. Posing
on a beach in Tripoli,
they watch as we undress.
Rigid, distant, and forever wounded,
your father stands in the center
like a soldier with his troops.
Nadia smiles. She is too young
to remember her banished brother.
Your mother holds a shell to her ear
and listens as if it is your voice
echoing across the Mediterranean. The shell
is dark, smooth and cut
open to the forces of the sea.
Your body still trembles, remembering

your mother's hand as it pressed
your face through the prison gates
to memorize it. The last night
your eyes search my body
as if it is unfamiliar.
We speak the wordless language
in your unheated room above
the blue and orange runway lights
where you whisper my name in Arabic
when your mind loves with your body.

I run a toenail along your arch.
Falaqua, you finally told me,
is a beating on the soles
of the feet. A punishment.
Fingering lines of the whip on your back
I feel the pain.
Scars are your body's language.

Tonight, I cannot touch you without crying.
While you sleep, I lie still,
watch the sky turning to ash,
tighten my fists around the leather
string of black beaded faith,
and I pray to my God to understand you.

To wake you, I touch
my lips to your forehead
as though you were a baby.
When you open your eyes, light
falls into my powerless hands.
And I take it.

Apparent Tranquility

It is reported that the former leader
of Uganda, Idi Amin, the man
responsible for killing half a million
of his own people, the man
whose favorite method of execution
was having two condemned people
beat each other to death with hammers,
lived in apparent tranquility
surrounded by family in a villa
near Jedda, Saudi Arabia.
Mr. Amin liked to fish and watch CNN.
He passed his time singing,
swimming, boxing, playing
the accordion and driving
around in a white Cadillac.

Slate

I run on gray roads
as silent and empty as slate
mines ringing this town.

Fog smears the mountains
until the colors
of the earth match

the colors of the sky,
and the winter air
thickens around me.

Something is shining
from the rusted
clutter of objects

someone calls home
at the bottom of a hill—
car parts, dirt colored trailer,

snowmobiles stuck in snow.
Santa's plastic sleigh
follows eight tiny reindeer.

Their yellow collars
blink like a warning.
A dog howls.

I disturb him
in the pit of silence
where he lives

at the end
of a rusty chain
tied to a trailer hitch.

I interrupt
the music of blue
sleet descending.

He hears me.
He greets me
like a wolf.

His teeth shine
like stars in the dark
cave of his mouth.

Sierra Snow

Above the thin trails that wander
through thimbleberry and thistle,
where mariposa lilies flow like cream
across miles of sage, and junipers
sprout from granite, as if all they need
lives in the sun-dried air,
stubborn summer snow still clings
to the mountainsides.

The river churns in the valley below,
blood flowing through a boundless heart.

The Sound of Snow

A swift sparrow, gray as the winter sky
it inhabits, flies into the boughs

of an evergreen and stays all morning;
the elms around it shake their last

dry leaves into the swirling
snow-filled air. Now the solitary

trill of the bird ascends,
and her heart enters the silence.

Newlyweds

A bride beneath a backpack
bigger than her body, holds
a vase of red and yellow
roses in front of her heart.
The groom, dragging a suitcase
on wheels, hugs a shopping bag
stuffed with still-wrapped gifts.
Wedding cake balanced on top.
Ribbons, spilling thin white streams
through the air behind them,
as they travel home with all
they think they will ever need.

A Normal Life

Whatever that is.
I don't pretend to know.

Don't think I haven't
tried to fold the socks

in neat pairs and stacked
the chipped blue rimmed bowls

and matching plates
inside the cupboard.

For years I have fed
the black and white dog

who barks whenever
the doorbell rings.

I filled the calendar
with important dates,

snipped daisies
blooming in the garden

beside the house, arranged
them in a glass vase

sitting in sunlight
on the kitchen windowsill.

Japanese Landscape

in Hokusai's *Mountainous Landscape*
with a Bridge dark birds circle
the tallest peak like footprints
leading to a valley hidden
by muddy hills dissolving
on a flood plain where a bridge
descends into a cluster of red
roofs tucked in a cedar grove
the sun sets on mountains
beginning to flame red
is the color of a woman
but the fine calligraphy
flowing through clouds
like strands of rain
is painted the color of dirt

Spring

After the rain, outside
the barred windows
of the classroom
tiny black birds
are bathing in puddles
beneath the oak trees.
Dipping into the icy water,
they shake their feathers
with such joy that their song
pulls us from our seats—
out onto the steps
where my students and I
walk into the first sunlight
we've felt for days
to watch them dance.

The birds remind me
of the Chinese peasants
I read about in college.
Sitting in the sunshine
on the first day of spring,
after cutting the quilted
clothes they were sewn
into for the long winter,
they gathered outside

to pick fleas from the sour
cotton lining of their jackets
and flick them at each other;
ducking and laughing
in the bright air,
while their children
ran naked into a pond
filled with melting snow.

On All Sides Water

We walk on planks fallen
over rising water,

weeks of winter rain,
streams on the dirt road winding

through the swamp that fills
then floods then fills again.

Drizzle drifts through
the roof of loblolly

branches. You name
the trees as if they were old friends—

sassafras and sweet gum,
tupelo and sugarberry.

At the lake raindrops spread
in concentric rings

rippling outward. It feels
like we are watching music

being composed. That's how it is
with us, joy in the rain,

the road back
washing away beneath our feet.

Sandur

Skeidararsandur, Iceland

Glacier-fed islands of
black volcanic glitter
form in the North Atlantic
overwash of ice and waves.

As scallop-edged triangles
lay their bodies down
on blue-patched lavender

seas, layers
of winter storm beat
against their twisted backs

until they flood,
flow, then flood again.
On this broad fan

the sand scatters, stretching
its dark shapes seaward, from the great
melting miles behind it, from Skeidarar
the top of the world.

Despite Gravity

They come from France, Sweden, Mexico and Maine.
Designers and engineers cradling blueprints
and calculations in their arms; ironworkers
wearing hard hats and steel-toed boots, sledgehammers
  grasped
in the grip of their gloved hands. With scars and sweat
drying on their skin, they come with memories
of the sea and gorges sliced between mountains;
rivers with forgotten names moving beneath them,
time rushing overhead, and the knowledge of birds
flowing in their blood. On a boat before dawn
they cross the water. Starlight washes over them.
The air is moist and cool. And they are silent.
They are grateful for the silence. All day
it stays with them, as they work at the edge of the sky.

They come, because a bridge is like a dream
of what is possible. It rises from the earth
as if gravity was something imagined,
and the forces of the universe were suspended.
Workers take plywood and steel, construct a framework
into the endless air, where cables holding
a million pounds of iron and concrete
are as elegant as the strings on a harp
playing the sounds of wind rising off water.

Poems from The Endless
Repetition of an Ordinary
Miracle

What Shines

Tears falling that no one sees   familiar
voices   voices you love and the bells
ringing at the end of day   seedlings
sprouting on the windowsill   the future
fish scales   iced branches   after
the storm   a choir   cloud covered stars
everyone's soul   white candles glowing
at the church entrance   desire   unspent
coins in a saucer   hair filled with sunlight
or water   what the diamond means

What If

the coin landed on heads instead of tails
wind blew in another direction
a boat landed here   the storm turned north
the car stopped before the patch of black ice
the fire never spread through the house
the bomb never dropped   the bullet missed its mark

What if grass was worshipped and Bach prevailed
Bonheoffer had succeeded   Europeans
had revered the Indians   angels were
visible   war was a memory
everyone forgot   what if the light
within us found a way to burn bright

What Passes

The old man in a plaid pressed shirt
walking two Scotties around the traffic circle
pick-ups bursting with Mexican lawn workers
a Buddhist monk in Nikes and a baseball cap

clumps of housewives on cell phones   a stream
of white kids   wet hair in clumps peddling home
from the pool   towels damp   clinging
to their necks like rigging holding them down

in the fume filled wind   trucks grinding
at the edges of the neighborhood   a swirl
of sulphur   butterflies   sirens in the distance
the tragedy of a stranger's life unfolding

a beaten wife with the phone in her hand
flattened carcasses of squirrels   unseen
alligators   a box turtle on its long trek to the pond
the shy widower watering roses in the dark

too many drunks behind the wheel   that loneliness
clouds wandering the sky like lost objects   or found
dreams of young boys on skateboards   complacency
never enough compassion or birdsong

What Remains

white feathers   in the nest   like a dusting of snow
emptiness of birth   after prayers   paint drying
on the canvas   it is raining   blue egg
in a glass   Jim Crow hidden in their hearts
a city divided   scars   in every home   the Gospel truth
at the bottom of an empty puddle   silence
when the last breath has been taken   days scratched
on the prison wall   shreds of silk   and sunlight
lining the abandoned   chrysalis   after the storm
the broken house   floating like a boat   a voice
filled with bells   a bed of leaves   ashes
on the mantel   history is the container
buried beneath the killing fields   a white string
still tied to a baby's wrist   and bones   clinging
together   across the miles   in the hotel of stars
iron and straw   a field of winter   fields of milk
the permanence of snow   and the arithmetic
after childhood   that sack of small stones
we carry   a heart filled with scars   the sea
holding too many bones   despite genocide
so many creatures in the air   fluttering
over the graves   and the onion domes
inside   memories of what is found there

Old Burial Hill

It is good to walk through old cemeteries
and count small white headstones
of the babies and mothers who died
giving birth; soldiers and fishermen
who fought the British, lying inches away.

It is good to rub your hands over
worn letters carved into gravestones,
consider the collective suffering
of these families, then listen
to the silence of stone. It is good

to go down to Red's Pond and feed
stale chunks of bread to the ducks,
then watch the old men race little wooden boats
on Sunday mornings and feel
as if my grandfather and father were still

standing on either side of me. Each one
holding my hands the way they would
in winter, when they guided me across
the frozen pond until I let go and skated
across the ice without them. It is good

to wander the curved narrow roads
of Old Marblehead, past crowded rows
of well-kept captain's homes
and street gardens filled with roses
draped across white wood fences.

At the bottom of the hill, vines weave
through frayed stacks of lobster pots
heaped high beside the fish houses
at Gas House Beach. A hundred years ago,
lobsters washed-up on the sand in piles,

pots overflowing and bursting.
My grandfather fed claws to chickens
and tossed the shells back to sea. At low tide
you can walk to the island on a thin trail
of slick rocks, worn glass, feathers, and blue-

black mussel shells; watch the boats set sail—
gulls gathered on the rigging like snow.
The low groan of the horn is the sound
of my childhood. As I walk the rim
of the harbor, fog trails the edges of morning.

The air is tinged with gasoline, salt, fish.
Like a lid slid over the harbor,
the uninterrupted slate sky
is the color of graves and winter sea.
There is nothing easy about this history.

But it is good to remember where you come from.
At the top of Fort Sewall I face Children's Island.
Seagulls skim the rocks. Someone is playing
bagpipe music across the Sunday morning stillness
My father is trying to tell me something.

Charleston Rooftops

Everything that lifts into the air
has purpose: even the granite tipped war
monument rising above palmetto trees
points like an arrow toward the sun;
chimneys, stove pipes, weather vanes and steeples—
the flag at half mast, flapping in the wind.

Streets clog with memories of smoke tinged wind—
of a dark sky on fire fueling the air,
flames swirling around steeples,
and a harbor blocked by ships of war.
Cannons fired toward the ever present sun
until the avenues lined with oak trees

were abandoned, and the trees
thrust transcendent into the wind
reached like prayers toward the sun.
Odors of ruin and rot lingered in the air
above the streets emptied by war;
the bells silent in the steeples.

Beyond scaffold enshrouded steeples,
sunlight weaves through leaf-thick oak trees
now filled with blossom and song, though war

saturates the brick and memory of wind
spinning with salt through summer air
that simmers beneath the blood streaked sun.

Red runs through ribbons of sun
across the skyline and steeples
lifting off tin sloped roofs into air
filled with flowering trees.
Always the tireless ocean wind
ripples the worn-out flags of war.

The names of the enemy change, but war
is the inscrutable language spoken beneath this sun.
The flag at half-mast, stiffens in the wind.
Funeral bells sound from the steeples.
In the cemetery, beneath the oak trees,
taps linger on the broken air.

The sounds of war will rumble in the wind.
As steeple bells call through the sun filled air,
birds nest in trees twisting toward heaven.

Boat People

In Geneva, where everything's labeled
in five languages, words take on imagined
meanings. In 1979, Pol Pot seemed
like a misspelled name for a cooking dish,
and the news from Asia was getting tiresome.
In this tidy city built at the edge
of a lake, stories surfaced in a continuous
stream. After days of listening
to starved, scarred Cambodian refugees
describe the genocide they barely survived,
I rode on the back of a motorcycle
to Montreux where Herbie Hancock and Chick Corea
were playing duets on a red oriental carpet.
On stage, in the swirl of spot lights and smoke,
their pianos faced each other. At first
they seemed like boxers in a ring, then more
like lovers, laughing through the charged air passing
between them. After a while the music
was like a fruit split in half in my mouth,
the sharp and flat of one note becoming whole
within me. I listened, with my stoned Swiss friends,
until I forgot the cruel cacophony
of stories I wish I had never heard. That morning
a lice covered boy described how soldiers
sliced his mother's breasts off with an ax.

She was going to have a baby he said
between bites of a chocolate bar.
She was tired all the time and couldn't
work quickly enough. His voice was soft
and steady. As he spoke, he watched swans
gliding across the lake outside the office window.

That night, Herbie Hancock was smiling
like he had never known such horror,
but it must be the opposite—
all that joy tumbling out of sorrow.

In Gaza's Berry Fields

Layers of clouds have cooled the air
until the paths beside rows of strawberry plants
are filled with families. Children run
around the edge of the field, tossing handfuls
of berries into white plastic buckets and each other—
hands and mouths stained pink with juice.

A woman straightens up to rest her back.
She looks for her sons who helped
all morning. They're playing marbles
with their friends near the roadside,
tracing circles in the dirt with a sharp stick,
taking aim and shooting fast. Their laughter
floats through the sky until it reaches her.

Something hot passes over her head. It feels
like her hair is on fire, but she knows the sound
of mortars and the smell that follows.
Before she has time to run and grab her sons, a shell
explodes in the middle of the berry field. The sky
fills with smoke and a brief hard silence.

A tank rolls past. Shredded bodies are scattered
across the strawberry fields. The soldiers gather parts
into piles near the road, where the boys were

playing marbles. The mother runs, tearing at
her white head scarf, as she moves through the path
in the middle of the berry field. The head
of her youngest son is on the greenhouse roof.

She pulls it down, kisses it, puts it in her lap,
and wraps it in her scarf. A hand is caught
in a tree above the greenhouse. She grabs it,
kisses the fingers, places the hand beside the head,
ties the ends of the white cloth into a tight knot
and holds the bundle to her breast. Blood begins

to spread across the fabric. Her middle son's torso
lies in the dirt near the piles of body parts. Legs
are lined up beside it. She picks up a small leg
with a sandal still attached. Wiping away the blood,
she kisses the toes and puts the foot in the bundle
she will hold against her body forever.

She sits down against the wall and tries to lift
her arms toward heaven. Her hands are chopping
the smoke in front of her, as if they can show
how her children were torn apart, or how
her heart feels. When a soldier walks by,
she grabs the end of his rifle and points it

at her belly. The soldier is young,
but older than her sons, who were just
playing marbles at the edge of a field
on a winter morning in January in Northern Gaza,
while their mother filled the last bucket of the day
with sweet, ripe strawberries.

Nocturne 2006

I

Owls call from the hollows.
This is the sound of the moon.

Light shattering like glass
across the night. Sky

filled with ghosts. They have
traveled far. This room holds

their voices like a box
of cracked bones. I remember

how to write my name
in a swirl of Arabic.

It is a secret. Sound,
like the sound of my name

in the halls where I walked
through moonlight, stepping

over soldiers facing Mecca.
The faces of the tortured are

familiar. Beneath hoods, a voice
I recognize. A muscled thigh, feet

in shackles, buttocks and kneecaps.
Skin smelling of sweat and urine.

II

A man is named for a prophet.
He calls for him in the darkness.

Naked and cold in a cage,
his middle name is God.

What the Shrine Wants

Beneath prayer flags strung across the top
of the windowpane, beside the arc
of baleen shredding in the corner
balanced against a red candle squeezed
into a glass stickered with blue eyed Santa Barbara
holding a chalice in one hand, sword
in the other, who is, according to the text painted
along the side—*a sublime and generous
protector*—on the white shelf
where the Buddhist shrine holds
photographs of the departed, prayer cards,
funeral programs, feathers and stones;
a small brown bird leaps like a fish
against the window. Over and over
in the light that hovers around this cluster
of souls, a small bird keeps rising
until he rests among the sweet faces,
the bleached shark vertebrae, birch bark,
sage bound in blue string and one stone
rubbed smooth in an earthquake.

Illuminata

Day One

On the first day of chemo
unexplained gifts appear on the doormat—
lavender soap wrapped in tissue paper,
a thick bar of dark chocolate and a quartz
sparkled rock to keep you earthbound.

Day Two

The saints must be busy today.
That's okay. You watch patterns of sun-
light slide across your bedroom wall.
The dog sleeps on top of your bed
and watches you carefully.

Day Three

Dried leaves in a pile woven together
by spider webs on the brick steps
have no meaning. But they hold
your attention for too long. Sleep now,
and wait for something green to appear.

Day Four

Late last night, your sister phoned.
You don't ask what took her so long,
because her voice is the one that answers
in dreams. It is the flame
singing through the longest night.

Day Five

Sunflowers tied with yellow velvet ribbon
greet you when you open the front door.
Peaches in a brown bag, a box of pastries
tied with a string, and bowl full of tomatoes.
The note is from a neighbor you hardly know.

Day Six

New copies of PEOPLE and VOGUE stacked
beneath a bottle of bright pink nail polish
the sticky note attached—"Something to do!"
"2 DVD's that will make you LAUGH—
"Pink Panther" and "A Fish Called Wanda."

Day Seven

After smoking the joint that was hidden
in an envelope labeled JUST IN CASE,
you look up the word *grace* in the dictionary.
"Thank you for the gifts," you write,
"I feel like a Saint has visited my doorstep."

Nothing Can Contain You

Not the wreath woven from fresh flowers,
nor the photograph it rings. Not the calm
smile at the center. Not the messages
inscribed by the ones who loved you most.
Not your initials, nor the dates
marked in black lettering across the white
cross, planted behind the guard rail
at the edge of a Georgia highway—
the one perpetually filling with sunlight.

But birds . . . .there should be birds.
Small and many. Birds that have just come
from the sea, which can't be far. There should be
one for each year. They should descend in a rush
and surprise, and smother the small trees
growing in a line beyond the roadside
memorial. They should be white. And from
a distance, it would look like a line of crosses
trembling beneath a sky full of sadness, full of song.

Pine Pitch

Clustered around the edges
of my father's open grave,
the grown-ups lean into one
another like bunches of crows,
pressing their pale wet faces
against the emptiness
of the slate sky gathering
in the late winter wind.
The flapping minister's robes
sound like sails unfurling
beside the coffin. It is
as if this man carries
the sea inside of him,
the way my father did.

Pine boughs cover the coffin.
Arranged like flowers from one
end to the other, they fill
the air with Christmas smells.
I think of my uncle, climbing
at dusk through falling snow
to do the one thing he could
still do for this man he loved

like a brother. I consider
the tenderness and courage
it must have taken to tear
the branches one by one,
from the mountainside. And how,
when his arms were full of pine,
he ran stumbling down
the trail he had made alone
through the woods. His hands covered
in dark patches of pitch
that stayed on his skin for days.

Spaghetti

Aunt Barbara was a beauty queen. Competing in the Miss
  America Pageant
and riding on top of floats in holiday parades in South Paris
  Maine
did nothing to prepare her for being a wife. When she was
  first married
to Uncle Buddy she knew how to boil water and cook
  spaghetti,
but the sauce was simply too much for her. So, she mixed
  catsup
into a little hot water left at the bottom of the pot,
poured it over the pasta, tossed in a lot of Kraft Parmesan
  Cheese
and served it almost every night. Uncle Buddy ate bowlfuls
of the stuff for months and told her it was delicious.
When my grandfather told me this story, he said
it's the kind of thing that happens when you really fall in love.
It was a summer evening. He was sitting in the Adirondack
chair behind the driveway in front of the railroad tracks
that ran through the yard behind my grandparent's house.
He smoked his pipe and talked while I pulled rhubarb from
  the garden.
We were waiting for Uncle Buddy and Aunt Barbara
to come in for the weekend, with my teenage cousins
who had long straight black hair and jeans so tight they had
  to lie down

on the bed to zip them up. On Saturday night, they played 45s
out in the shed and danced with the local boys.
And if we hadn't bothered them too much during the day,
the would let me and my cousins watch them through the
    window
and dance to Elvis and the Beatles out on the grass;
my grandparents sitting back in their chairs watching us,
tapping their feet and clapping until the train roared through
    town.

My Quaker Grandmothers

It is 1900, and my grandmother has arrived
in the middle of July like a new planet in the sky.

Firstborn and adored, she is dressed
in a long white cotton gown for the photograph.

While she sleeps, she curls her fist
around her mother Marion's index finger.

Marion, seated like a queen in a throne,
holds my grandmother's face toward the camera.

Married to a railroad Baron, my great grandmother
wants for nothing in the world. But she is Quaker,

and what she wants she already has. There are stories
about refusing jewels and elaborate gifts; no wine

in the home, only a bottle of whiskey for snake bites;
books overflowing in the library; a garden

of old English roses, rosemary, and mint growing
beside the sprawling house built purposely in the shade.

Marion's mother and grandmother stand stiffly
on either side of the chair. Their starched black dresses

cover everything but their grim faces. Hair tied back
into knots, heads covered in white bonnets—

no one is smiling on this joyous occasion.
The women look down toward my grandmother

the way all eyes look toward Christ
in certain nativity paintings. The ones

where the angels bow their heads, and the infant
is the only one facing the heavens.

Stillborn

Blue jays zigzag through leafless
black branches at the edge of
the winter field where a cow
has lain three straight days, since
birthing a stillborn calf.
When she moans, the cry comes from
the great gulf of grief that is
motherhood. One tree trembling,
alone; red berries on tips
of the tallest branches,
this is what the cow sees
through air, the color of tears.

Annunciation

the Archangel is expected   almost
kneeling   robes flowing like water

against the late afternoon   silence
dominating   the room's internal

order   in the corner   Mary
paused in prayer   head down

hesitant   wrapped in blue wool
she sits beneath a dove   ringed by fire

such resistance in the air
not the room   as the pattern

is certain   long rectangled
windows   holding daylight

the floor   composed of diamonds
gray and brown   squares

red   white starred   red
dress   the bed draped in silk

square white pillow at rest
such stillness   at the center

of this story   *fleur de lys*
in bloom   the world outside

the window   diminished
as the room transforms into a kind

of reliquary   everything
sacred   swirling towards night

Seeking

It happens in stillness. Because it is night
you hear snakes drop from the oak
and other things you can not name
passing beneath or above you. Trees
so thick the stars are mute.
Close your eyes. The immensity
of such unquantifiable light
fills the emptiness that once was
memory. After the hunger
and solitude, dreams and the dead
speaking as if they are with you,
it happens when the oak begins to burn
from within. And you welcome the flames.

Spring Island, South Carolina

beyond clusters of dark birds   hovering
at the edge of sky   the wind bends yellow
tipped marsh grass rippling around a rim
of sand   uninterrupted waves spilling
one on top of the other   as everything
spins into salt   into sunlight
houses rise like castles   built on sand
each home   an alchemy of conquest
fire   hope   for there is more
light than we can hold   the end always
flowing like water   what we become
in the diffusion of divinity   across
the blind distance   light emanates
from a flaming sky   this is the world
at war   the air is bright and blessed
but the land is bent by hands of fire   burning
where islands dream at the edge of sky

New Poems

Family Reunion

I want to pray, but the doors
to the gray stone church are locked.
Early morning and fog still
clinging to hilltops as if
something is hidden. But there
is a trail behind the church
calling me into the woods,
far from the sea, far from home.
It is cool and dark beneath
the dense trees, and the wind filled
with pine is slight but steady
against my skin. I make my way
along the path, past piles of stones
that might mean something to someone,
and occasional birches
standing alone. I am moving
into the future, but stumbling
through my past as I zigzag
up and down the maze of trails
carved into the place I come from.
Few birds and one startled doe
pass before me. I smile
at no one and let the joy
of this encounter fill me
like music, but no voices

or distant trains echo
in this hallowed wood. Absence
is the thing that calls us back
to places emptied of
everything but remembrance.
My father taught me to listen
for God in the silence
of the earth, unencumbered
and filling with light.
This morning, the hornet's nest
hanging from a low beech branch,
where Maple Trail opens to
a logging road, could be a sign
of something ominous,
but there is a green stillness
brightening the air and church
bells chiming in the distance,
aunts and uncles walking
down the hotel stairs for breakfast,
cousins on the porch, waiting
for the sun, and plenty
of time to pray alone.

The Christmas Apron

Unfolding my grandmother's apron, tucked
deep in a box of Christmas decorations,
I rub my hands across the wrinkled
cream colored cloth as thin as gauze
and the bright red and blue boxes circling
the hem and see her standing at the stove
wearing her Christmas apron, stirring pots
on every burner, a turkey already roasting
in the oven, plates of gingerbread men
cooling on the counter. Each one her own
creation. Dozens of cousins, aunts, and uncles
circle the kitchen table in a haze
of coffee, bacon, and cigarettes. Damp wool
hats and mittens steam on the radiator
beneath the kitchen windows thick with frost.
My grandfather hauls in wood in from the shed,
smelling of pipe smoke and peppermints,
shaking fresh snow from his plaid flannel sleeves.

It's as if my childhood was inscribed
on this stained handful of cloth, scattered
with a celebration of ornaments
tied with green ribbon and a tiny tag pinned
at the waistband—This was Nana's apron.

Corene

summer flowing like a song
only she can hear   standing
in the tilting tall grass that is
singing also   a woman holds
a blue polka dot sheet
overhead   as if it is
a privilege to be   standing
in an open field   with wind
lifting her dress while she
dries baskets of clean laundry
beneath a sun filled sky

Easter Worry

This morning, the churchyard is covered
in a dusting of pollen as if a light snow
fell during the night, changing everything it touched.
And the world emerged thrumming and green.

Who knows what part the wind played or where
it comes from, how it swirls the bees into a lazy spin
above the garden and lifts the sparrows to their nest
on a window ledge beneath the eaves. The sky fills
with winged creatures, magnolia blossoms, sweet
notes of familiar hymns, and all the unutterable prayers—
for the child that never phones, the neighbor
with a spot on her lung, the father who cannot be pleased.

Much is said today about the meaning
of the mystery. I think of it as something
remembered then shared, like a small nest
holding everything we love.

Intersection Where the Rain Begins

wherever there is sand   gathering
beside water   black boulders
glistening above bright bunches
of bamboo   banana spiders
at work between overlapping
branches   weaving webs   like the outline
of arteries sprawled across a stranger's
exposed shoulders as the row
of prisoners crossing the narrow bridge
in a scribble of silence   watches
the jagged red leaves float   upriver
where someone is dancing   alone
locked on the edge   of a rock   as the world
of the waterfall explodes beside her
and it looks like the inside
of every cloud   gathering

Where a Mirage Has Once Been,
Life Must Be

in the blur of passing hours
accumulating   as perfect circles
light   green gold   odor
of river   rising   mud washed
slipper strewn   tinged   with moonlight
paused   for one undulating kiss

after love   their long bodies
rise from the earth   marsh grass straightening
behind them   marks that patch of joy
already   darkening   they stumble
through ripe fields of abandoned
rice   rippling   in the wet wind

toward the sea   where waves shape
stones   into piles   marking the edge
stillness   water   ribboned
violet blue layers   light
wrapping   unraveling
as permanent   as earth   imagined

or this day   stretching across   dreams
like smoke   swirling beneath them   and within

When All the Branches Overlap

It is time to trim the vine
covered trees that camouflage
our house. Home to a world
of insects and birds whose songs
awaken us and lull us
to sleep, whose ceaseless circling
through thick summer air
is not some lazy journey
under the sun, but the work
that fills their days with purpose.
And the music that they make
is part of that, so we listen
in our chairs, resting in the shade
made by overlapping branches
of oak, fig, magnolia,
and banana. Let the fruit
continue to ripen
and the flowers bloom
in their orange pots.
Let the fallen leaves remind
us of the days we can never
get back. Let these tall trees
stand for marriage, the place we
made out of shade and sunlight.

A Place for You

Take time to hover at the still
mouth of this ancient harbor
then rise into the air, which holds

a place for you. Let the wind
off the sea lift you up and hold
you above the daily cacophony,

before your hours fill
with unintentional clutter,
the way small clouds seem

to occupy the sky on days
you are not paying attention.
Do not ignore the ordinary—

each drop of gray drizzle,
every stone and snapped twig,
all the creatures, thriving here.

Because there are questions
with no answers and many days
you will wish to forget,

savor each hour of sunlight
when it permeates the sky,
streaming through you

like music. Listen to the glittering
wings beating within
the engine of your heart.

The Weight It Takes

In the white silence that is winter
return to the river, if only
for solitude. Begin at the roots.
Touch the pulse that keeps
flowing on its own. Sometimes
you will need only this.

For rivers are just a way for us
to find one another. Each rock,
the weight it takes to keep us
here; the fish, just fleeting
friendships, that will disappear
and reappear when we least expect it.

Beneath a tangle of trees,
the riverbank is an altar
holding water; the single vessel
taking in miles of spinning leaves,
lost feathers, and the dreams
of all who come here.

Now your life belongs to the world.
Hold fast to everything
beating with sunlight.

Pull us together, like water.
Be the weight that grounds us
through swirling hours of each day.
When voices shout without ceasing,
be the stillness we hear ringing in our hearts.

As Dreams Unwind

A sliver of moon burns
through the bedroom skylight

before dawn. The air is cold
and filling with silence.

The winter winds have stopped
swirling across the stars.

and the vast trees trembling
in the night are still.

Time, which was once
vague and incalculable,

spreads like snow
through an empty sky.

The Top of the World

"Out in the yard, a doll without arms, a tricycle
with a missing back wheel. Nothing seemed
whole."

Ron Rash, The World Made Straight

A blue tube stretches between
maple trees, like clothesline strung
along the path to the top
of the world. In spring it will
fill with thick sap and flow
to the sugarhouse below
on its journey from the stars.
At the top of the trail,
two white Adirondack chairs
with hearts carved into their backs
face mountains that ring this town
with impossible snow. Clouds
hide the tallest peaks. The sweep
of pines spreads in waves flowing
as far as we can see,
punctuated with houses
and chimney smoke and stillness.
At night, their lights are candles
flickering on a winter

altar. In the clearing
at the top of the world,
abandoned cars and tractors
are stuck in ice. Two trailers
hover at the edge of the woods
as if they are waiting for
passengers. A rocking horse
sits in an orange metal frame
tipping head-first into ice.
In the center of the field;
a gas grill is half buried
in snow. Beside it, the torn
carcass of a deer in shreds.
Two sets of coyote tracks
lead into the woods, but the silence
of the missing is the only
sound we hear. It was summer
once, and the waterfalls gushed
white and cold all day long.
At the swimming hole we drank beer,
jumped from cliffs and raced up the trail
to the top of the world. At night
we built bonfires, told stories
filled with lies, and made love
in the back of a hunter's trailer
while Nirvana sang on the radio.
Occasionally a gun
was fired into the air.

Daybreak, John's Island, South Carolina

Winter feels like a stranger, sleeping
in a darkened closet at the back
of an old house, where faucets drip all night.
And the wind, furious and gray, whirls
through the sky, disrupting the possibility
of dreams. In fields at daybreak
rows of migrant workers,
standing on ladders, break open
iced peach buds; their breath
rising and resting above the fields like clouds.

Snow in the South

rarer than rainbows   hurricanes
or hail   startling
how this snow   fell   once
in decades   that came
and went as fast as this   winter
dream   then stayed
clinging in clumps   on
shaded sides of the highway
despite midnight drizzle
and morning sun   so many snowballs
rolled out across cold fields
of cotton   snowmen stacked
in front of every home   around
the edges of town   that night
the hip-hop singer   dj
named Buddha   preacher
in a pressed black suit   fiery wings
in a metal tray   above a bowl
of blue flame   that tall cousin
with the little boy   hip to ankle
nigerian pink tie-dye   leaning
on one crutch   her bright smile
on stage   baraka beating

the side of the podium
with a flat palm   still full
of hard earned anger
wool scarf wrapped tight around
his neck like some kind of armor

Forgotten

As long as songbirds call back and forth
across the morning stillness, as if the sun
came pouring from their trembling throats
in streams of spoken light, the day will come.
And we will enter, although our hearts lie
tangled deep in beds of grief. All night,
horned owls haunted the empty edge of sky—
until their endless echo marked our lives.

Between the tallest reach of pine and cloud,
swallows glide in overlapping circles,
the way a mind revolves around a wound
too deep to heal. Rising from this sleepless swirl,
we walk onto the dampened earth, to bury
memories of things no bird can see.

In Sorrow and Sunlight

In memory of Carrie Levenson-Wahl

On her last day, I was driving south
Past fields of corn and cotton; miles of green
Sloped hills where horses roamed between small towns,
Like memories of places I'd never been.

Once, I drove across mountains to see her.
Horses grazed in the fog filled fields beside
Her house, moisture clinging to their fur—
Like strings of tiny stars shining in sunlight.

In my dreams she lives, within the world she loved.
Notes ringing the morning air like tears—
Her voice tinged with sorrow and sun,
The bell song of her leaving filling the spheres.

And this is what I hear calling in the night,
When stars remind me of her joy and her bright
Suffering, my friend singing in the gathering light.

The Art of Memory

in the blue hour   I wake
to remember   you   this day
in the heart of winter   sunlight
slowly seeping into a corner
of the sky   and I   continue
to pray   through decades in which
I have become   more
fatherless   but less alone
I can not explain   how
this happened   or why
I sense the mutable
interior of things   thriving
hidden   humming with life
like houses   lit up at the dinner hour
or letters written   even the stones
we stumble   over   here
beyond this color   filling
the air   there is nothing but
memory   restless   wandering
stars that fade   somewhere
in the back of the mind   a kind of
music   I want   to gather
each hour that bears your name
like holding rain or counting waves

at the beach with my children
you'll never know   we watch
for birds   lost in the cacophony
of dawn   your voice   oblivion
a shadow   drawn across the sea

Winter Light

Out of the darkness lights blaze
above my neighbor's front door
but the house is empty.

Out of the silence birdsong
invisible but bright
as the winter moon.

Out of the still dawn a pause
in the order of things
rising imperceptibly.

Out of the silver shimmering
fog skimming the earth
this moment that was her life.

February Triptych

with winter   there are wounds   impossible
to heal   yet   everything   sings
backwards and blooming   palmetto
and pine   as if grown   from one root
the same green branches tossing outside
ten curtainless windows   of this seven cornered
room   so many walls   smoke white   like
scattered clouds   and the same colored shelves
with books   and sunlight   but no explanation
for this loss   only words   moving across pages
like loud geese   confused   in the winter winds
suddenly crisscrossing the late afternoon   sky

The Stones Beneath Our Feet

For Whitney Powers and Olive Gardner

Bless the crushed flowers cradled
in bright tissue paper tied
to a white bicycle
on a street running straight
to the sea. Bless the waves paused
in the harbor and our first
shared memory of water.
Bless the travelling voices
trapped in the air as if words
were something permanent
and bigger than stones
beneath our feet. All those small things
that carry us through the hours—
a straight line of pelicans
caught in sunlight, the ripe
orange on a blue plate, your
favorite book beside it,
jessamine winding itself
around worn windowpanes;
that sweet smell spinning through
the room until you're dizzy.
Bless each bird and turning page;
the perfect circle of rind,
piles of petals at your feet.

Summer Dirge

If there is rain, let it be
lead-blue, shattering like glass
across this gray morning sky.
Let it be salt-tinged and iced
with sea. Let it sting like tears
falling, today. As we gather
at your graveside, let it rain.

Undertow

encounter   the tempting thing   think
unfamiliar   go somewhere unexpected
ask   about the steeper slope   approach
on a slight angle   running beneath
when there is heavy action
get out   build up   and look
a weak point   push out   create a rip
which will carry you   knowing
this not the same   as   understanding
push towards   the hope   of tearing
through   a terrible idea   before
you reach   the best thing   return

you reach   the best thing   return
through   a terrible idea   before
push towards   the hope   of tearing
this not the same   as   understanding
which will carry you   knowing
a weak point   push out   create a rip
get out   build up   and look
when there is heavy action
on a slight angle   running beneath
ask   about the steeper slope   approach
unfamiliar   go somewhere unexpected
encounter   the tempting thing   think

Counting Scars

I

Born as the August sun pulsed
from the center of the sky
clearing every wisp of cloud
and piece of wind in a rush
of light that seemed to fill
the world, this small offering
drenched in water and blood
as if carried on a flood tide
from a great distance only
I have traveled, my fragile
bundle of woven bones
and wonder, opened one blue
eye and then the other, curled
his ten fingers into fists
at his sides, as if to say
I'm ready, and then a frown
traveled across his mouth
as he turned his head toward
the opening window.

II

The halo of light remained,
as I nursed him through
the litany of colds,

ear aches, chicken pox—germs, tossed
back and forth between brothers
as easily as Frisbees.
Holding him tight at every
painful corner: sharp splinters,
sunburns, jelly fish sting;
not letting go until the torn
skin was stitched, and the throat
turned pink as a rose. Only
the body grown around these scars
would remember any of it.
But the mind, rumbling
beneath his skull like a cloud
unraveled at the edge of sky,
held the wound that tried to break
his life apart—unnamable
and unutterable.

III

Waterboy sprung from the sea,
return whenever you feel
a longing for something
luminous you cannot name.
When turtles swim through your sleep
follow them into the deep,
though it is dark and difficult
diving into those places
of multiplying silence.

Because your home was built
on a narrow mound of sand
held down by wandering vines,
where turtles dig deep holes
into the dunes for nests,
the eggs they will abandon

with blind hope and the kind
of faith we all hunger for,
return with flipper and wing,
scales that sparkle near the sun-
lit surface of the sea, to float
beneath a blur of clouds,
letting black sand spill slowly
from your opening hands.

Brainstorming

Nothing could be further from their minds
than summer. As cold rain streaks the floor
to ceiling classroom windows,
I make them close their eyes and listen
to the poem "Knoxville, Tennessee."
A place none of us have visited,
but we find it on the map taped
beside the door. It's not too far from here,
they like that. It's near the mountains,
a tiny girl named Nicole says,
as she runs her finger along the Great Smokies
I've never seen a mountain, she sighs.

Yesterday, we wrote about memories—
the first ones that came to mind. After
Tinesha described sleeping in the bathtub
every night since the drive-by shooting
that killed her big brother, the stories
pour on to the paper in a torrent. Tears
for the father who came back from the desert
in a casket, the mother in jail,
two hours away in Columbia,
the real reason for Dante's broken arm,
gunfire at the playground and the funerals
that followed, the uncle who spit on his

niece's bare belly before walking out
the door after raping her Thanksgiving
night, and the mother who told her
daughter to forget about it.

Today we will remember sunlight,
long train trips to visit cousins,
squirt gun fights, video games and staying up
late. Nicole wants to hear the poem again.
While they listen to descriptions
of *barbecue and buttermilk,*
homemade ice cream at the church homecoming,
rain hits the glass hard and steady.
All that talk about food, makes them hungry.
After you make a list of nouns
you associate with summer,
we'll go to lunch, I promise. Brainstorm.
Whoever makes the longest list wins
a prize. Leonard, who is already
bigger than half the men I know, but young
enough to carry a raggy blanket
at the bottom of his Batman backpack,
raises his hand first. He has written the word
bikini beside the lines about
going barefoot and being warm,
I know I won't win the prize, he grins,
but that's my dream of summer.

A Sisyphean Task

Photographs from Port-au-Prince, September 12, 2010

1.
city of crushed concrete
caving in from its core gray
heaped   busted-up   cracked slab
half a wall   cinder block   flipped
upside down   imploding
spilling bricks   along the streets
to the cockeyed palace
rock mounds reaching the sky
2.
a middle aged man
wearing torn jeans sweaty T-shirt
and sandals   skin covered
in a fine layer of dust
spends his days clearing rubble
with a rusty shovel
and wheelbarrow—
he was an artist once

A Monstrous Terrible Story

I

"There is no future here."

Alexander Tveretinov, age 57

Stray dogs wandering dirt roads,
tumbledown houses, closed
copper mine flooded with old
rain and rust. Everyone
drunk by noon in Lyovikha.
Just more human flotsam
in the riptide of despair
that sets into northern
villages built at the edge
of forests stretching towards ice,
where winter lasts eight months,
and the sun stays buried
beneath clouds, the color of loss.

II

"... he doesn't want them to steal."

Nadezhda Kirillova, age 70

Every morning, young men wander
in from the woods, red eyed,
silent and smelling of smoke.
There is a church with a priest
at the gate handing out coins
for bottles of cough syrup
and cheap wine; small pensions
mailed to the aged; every day
another villager dies.

III

"That story unmasked the truth"

Vadim Dubichev, advisor to the governor.

Five years ago, a stray dog
nosing around in the woods
discovered the decomposing
bodies of fifteen young girls
from a nearby city. Missing
for years, the police did little
to find them. Perhaps the men
had ties to the gang that kidnapped
the girls and forced them into a life
of prostitution; perhaps
they feared retribution;
more likely they just didn't care.

IV

"There is no need for people here anymore."

Alexander Tveretinov

On Sunday, a young fisherman
stumbled on to a row
of industrial-sized barrels
in the woods surrounding
his hut. He was a bit lost
when he discovered them,
and as soon he stopped to see
the contents, he wanted to run.
But his feet seemed suddenly
disconnected, the way his voice
sometimes disappeared from fear.
Scattered at his feet and spilling
out of the barrels were hundreds
of curled human fetuses,
tags marked with the last name tied
around their wrists and ankles.

V

"Why not give them to the fire, or the earth?"

Nadezhda Kirillova

There's no end to the mystery
of this gruesome discovery.
The fetuses, too big
to have been aborted, could have
been intended for some sort
of medical procedure;
maybe they were stillborn.
No one knows how they ended up
tossed into barrels like garbage

and left out for the birds
and animals to eat, deep
 in the Siberian forest,
near a forgotten village,
but everyone there knows
it has to do with money
or the lack of it.

Rain Coming From a Bright Sky

Photograph #34585 Nazi officers and female auxiliaries
(Helferinnen) pose on a wooden bridge in Solahutte. July 1944.

I

Caught by something unexpected
as sudden summer rain
in a place where everything
astonishes: the cool lake
that seemed to be waiting for them
when they stepped down off the bus,
Eiderdown pillows and quilts
in every sunlit bedroom,
afternoon chocolates with wine
the color of gold. All of it
like a continuous dream
of home, as if the river
carried these things to Solahuette,
for the women of the SS
and uniformed officers
posed on a wooden bridge,
laughing like little children
as the accordion player,
the one still wearing a cap,
played a familiar tune.
Giddy and giggling

they threw up their hands and ran
toward the alpine lodge, tucked
into the sloping wooded hills
on the outskirts of Auschwitz,
stopping just long enough
for a photograph, despite
mud filled shoes and drizzle
dampened hair, because they were young,
on holiday, waiting for
evening, beer and cigarettes
on the terrace under the stars,
dreaming of romance, because rain
seemed just right for Solahutte.
Because they were far away
from the office and telephones,
piles of paperwork, bad coffee,
endless orders from Berlin;
far from barbed wire fences
humming with electricity,
guard dogs, gunshots at the Black Wall,
and pistols echoing
through the long night. Gone were rows
of white barracks, the masses
of prisoners—their stench,
their cries, incomprehensible
mumbling, mindless stumbling;
far from the crematorium,
broken down from overuse,
and the smell of bodies
burning in open pits.

II

It didn't matter how loud
they sang around the fireplace
after dinner or how many
doors were shut tight in the lodge;

the low rumble of trains
travelling from all directions
at every hour, lifted
from the pines like music
playing in the background
of every room at Solahutte.
This long note of human
suffering would stay and hum
inside them, not only when
trains passed through their village,
but in odd quiet moments
that would comprise their long lives,
while standing in the field behind
the house, for example,
pinning socks and damp sheets
to the clothesline, at the sink
washing carrots, or later
when heads bowed over for prayer
around the table. And after
in the darkness, there would be
no end to the noises, imagined
or otherwise. It doesn't
matter if it's actually
something heard, when the heart
quickens and the mouth goes dry.
That is when their memories
return to Solahutte,
and the first time they saw
a slow ripple spread across
the lake as transport trains passed
through the forest, and later
the sudden summer rain.

The Philosophy of Gardening

Wearing a white tank T-shirt tucked into black pants, Tony walks in circles around the edges of the garden. Pausing at the fence, he writes down everything he needs to do. All day, his wife Kasha scrubs floors and fills the clothesline suspended between the kitchen window and a pear tree. He stays outside—watering, pruning, and napping in the shade. He picks tomatoes for their lunch. When he hands them to her through the window, she rubs the numbers on his arm as if she could erase them. He barely feels her fingers on his skin, his hands still warm from the fruit he'd held for a long time like newly hatched eggs, his hands covered in soil and water.

While she washes and slices the tomatoes, Kasha watches her husband through the window. He is watering the newly planted grass and talking to it as if it wouldn't grow without him. She joins him outside. They eat the tomatoes, sausage, cheese, and sweet rolls from the Mexican bakery on 8th Avenue. Then, they sit together on lawn chairs beneath a green plastic roof their sons attached to the brick wall last spring. Sometimes they put the radio on the windowsill and listen to the Polish radio station. On Sunday afternoons when the grandchildren visit, they drink wine in little glasses and dance on the red cement patio.

But winter pushes them inside. Nights are long convoluted caves from which there is no escape. Like small explosions, light bulbs startle the darkness. An enormous evergreen blazes at Christmastime in the living room. Tony and Kasha sit on the beige couch for hours, watching the tiny white bulbs blinking on and off, on and off. Later, when they sleep, nothing bad can happen in this Brooklyn apartment where light is pouring from the windows all night.

Manacles

Little boys like to dig holes and play with weapons. Like it or not, there's no stopping this. It keeps them busy for hours. I watch my sons from the window of the renovated gate house where we live. Where we live, gate house is a fancy way of saying slave house. There's no gate houses where I grew up near Boston. My mother, who still lives there and watches *Antique Road Show,* says our backyard is a veritable treasure trove of metal memorabilia. Civil War coins and slave medallions worth more than the property that contains them. She even sent a metal detector one Christmas.

Today my sons, dressed in yellow toy hard hats, overalls, gloves and black rubber knee high boots are digging for buried treasure in the backyard. They have been to the pirate museum in Charleston, read the Poe story about Sullivan's Island, and made elaborate treasure maps on crinkled beige paper which indicate that gold can be found near the swing set. Within minutes they seem to have engaged half the neighborhood in the backyard digging project. They've agreed to share the treasure with anyone who helps them dig. Two weeks ago, in a neighbor's yard, they found a door with the knob still attached, pieces of a broken plate, and the skeleton of an animal, which they're certain is a werewolf. Most likely it's some kind of dog.

Whenever one of them yells, it means they've hit something hard. There's a lot of that going on now. They're in the house, and they are calling for me. Taylor, the littlest one, is holding up a set of muddy rusting manacles. He is only four, and he can barely keep them from dropping on the ground. I take them from him. In my hands, they are as heavy as bricks. It makes me feel queasy, holding them like that. They are that heavy. The older guys—Hunter, Stephen and Ryan, who think and act like they know everything, call them *slave handcuffs*. They're trying to convince the younger ones that *there's lots of money for stuff like this.* This isn't the treasure the little boys had in mind, however. And Taylor cannot be convinced that slavery could have ever happened here or anywhere else, for that matter. He doesn't know that much about cruelty. He hasn't started school yet, on the island where we live. He wants to call his Nigerian cousins right now and warn them about the bad guys from Charleston who have something to do with pirates, and could be, for all he knows, on a boat right now on their way to Africa to kidnap them and bring them to Sullivan's Island. The island where we live, the place where slaves were kept by the thousands before they were sold or buried, here in the backyard of the gatehouse still standing on the island where we live.

Louisiana's Disappearing Chains

Formed on the lacy fringes
of abandoned river lobes,
five chains of islands clinging
together, grew into
galaxies of sand spits.
Soon the water people came
by the thousands to grow
cotton and sugar cane, trap
and fish, build fine hotels
along the shores of *Grand Isle,*
where shrimp filled every net
thrown into the sea and oysters
grew so easily a man once
made an island by tossing
the sharp shells in layers around
his elevated home.
Pirates and smugglers
descended into the delta
hiding in unmapped waters
of Barataria Bay
until the Navy captured
them at Grand Terre.
Still they came, from Spain, France,
the Philippines, and Malay.

Cubans, Chinese, Cajuns,
freed slaves and Europeans.
Even when hurricanes roared
in from the Gulf, they rebuilt
their little towns on stilts,
although the dead usually
outnumbered the living.
Along the Mississippi
walls of levees and dikes
choke the river with sediment
that once flowed onto the islands
like layers of sunlight. As waves
rise and wear away the edge
of land, the shoreline retreats
and the marshes disappear.
The Timbaliers are sinking
despite seawalls, oil rigs,
and all the money in the world,
as the last of these islands
dissolve into the sea.

Teen Wears Pet Bird Like a Hat

When 16-year old twins Erin and Tammy Wallace
go shopping together; they're not hard to tell apart.
Erin is the one with the bird on her head.
Sunday, a brightly feathered sun conure,
likes to perch atop Erin's ponytail, clutching
a wad of brown hair in one claw, while using
her hair elastic to balance himself
with the other claw. Sunday holds tight—
on long walks on the beach, bike rides,
even when Erin does back flips. When Sunday
is not riding high, he perches on Erin's shoulder.
Leaning forward, he rubs his head
affectionately against her eyelashes.
Erin started training Sunday to socialize
by taking short trips to the grocery store
when he was six months old. She wanted him
to be comfortable with strangers, and try
not to bite them. People hold him in line
at the check-out, she said, it teaches him
I'm not the only person he can trust.

Runaway Cow Tracked Down in Germany

A cow named Yvonne, whose escape
kept a corner of Bavaria
on tenterhooks, has turned herself
in after three months on the run.
The brown dairy cow escaped
from a farm in May then hid
in the forest. A few days
later, she was involved in
a near collision with a police car,
and local authorities
labeled her a public danger.
The folks at the animal
sanctuary, which now owns
the errant bovine, said
a farmer called them to say
that Yvonne had shown up
on their farm in the Muehldorf
area near the Austrian border.
One of the employees
confirmed Yvonne's identity
with the help of her ear tag.
The six year old cow "apparently

got tired of the loneliness,"
the local councilman said
in a statement, adding
that she jumped over a fence
to join her fellow bovines.

Police Say Roving Cows
Drank Backyard Brews

A roving group of cows crashed
a small backyard gathering
in a Massachusetts town
where they bullied the guests
for beer. Boxford Police
Lieutenant James Riter says
he spotted them in a front yard
while responding to a call
for loose cows on Sunday.
The herd high-tailed it for
the backyard and then he heard
screaming. When he ran back there
the cows had chased off the young
adults and were drinking their beer
after knocking the cans over
on the table and lapping
up what they spilled. He says
they even started rooting
around the pile of empties
in the recycling bins
for a few extra drops.

The Way Sound Travels

Song birds evolved long before humans
were around to listen, but they don't sing
to charm us, though parrots share our thick tongues.
In fact, not all birds actually sing; their call-
notes are not true music, but rather
signals for courtship, copulation,
pleasure, alarm, distress. Flight calls
for beginning and ending the journey
or staying still, keep the flock coordinated.
Even the smallest chicks listen to their parents
from inside the eggs. Some birds sing
two different notes at once, especially males.
Females are turned on by such complexity.
Sound travels best at dawn, before the sun
heats the air, twisting each note into an echo.
Even something as tenuous as wind
can shift a note enough to confuse friends.

In My Light Year

The day is bright, the cardinal at the feeder
is brighter. Beneath the doorjamb, stray leaves
that slid in on the night wind, stick to the floor
like decorations. It is cool
in the unlit hallway. At the end,
behind the closed door, the artist fills her canvas
with gray; washing over waves, patches of grass,
and sunshine swimming through the air
as if the earth was merging with the sky.
The other side is black, with tracings
of a shape as if a ghost lived there.

I am walking down the middle, past
the nest made of twigs, moss, and long strands
of black horse tail hair sticking out from the sides.
Emptied of four gray tufted phoebe chicks,
the nest seems suddenly useless and sad.
I move on into the pasture, past
the brown horse with the white star on her forehead
and a single scratch on her back, dipped
over the knobby fence, chewing on tall grass
that grows beside the road, which is filling
with cows that won't budge, as I step over

the broken oak limbs blocking my path
until I find the cedar split open
in last night's storm, and touch the pink pulp
rising from its center as if the great tree
had given birth in the night.

Notes and Acknowledgments

"The Nest of Stars": The poem is dedicated to Luanne Smith Havlicek.

"How the Yellow Angels Hunger": This poem is dedicated to the memory of Timothy Michael Reese Jr.

"Irises": The poem is dedicated to my mother Mary Kneeland Heath.

"The Coming Light": The poem is inspired by photographs taken by Lauren Preller.

"Despite Gravity": The poem was written for the dedication ceremony and opening of the Arthur Ravenel Jr. Bridge, July 16, 2005, Charleston, South Carolina.

"Strip Search": The poem is dedicated to Shahid Nadeem.

"Dancing Barefoot in Atlanta": The poem is dedicated to Juan Mendez.

"Illuminata": The poem is dedicated to Jodi Novak.

"Pine Pitch": The poem is dedicated to my uncle, Jerry Smith.

"Annunciation": The poem was commissioned for a project at the Indianapolis Museum of Art. The painting is a *Triptych of the Annunciation, Master of the Legend of St. Ursula*. The poem is dedicated to Harriet Popham Rigney.

"What Remains": The killing fields refers to the sites where Cambodians were killed and buried by the Khmer Rouge regime, during the genocide between 1975 to 1979. In Hmong culture, a string is tied to a newborn's wrist on the third morning after birth in a soul calling ceremony. The white string insures that the baby's soul will stay in the body

"In Gaza's Berry Fields": The poem is based on Steven Erlanger's article "In Gaza's Berry Fields, a Family Reels After Losing 7 Boys to Israeli Fire" from the *New York Times*, January 7, 2005.

"Nothing Can Contain You": The poem was commissioned by Ken Daniels for his film *David's Cross*. The poem is inspired by the roadside memorial for David Hilderbrand, who was killed in a car accident as a teenager near Savannah, Georgia.

"Family Reunion": This poem is dedicated to my aunt and uncle, Suzanne and Rupert Grover.

"Corene" and "Seeking": Poems inspired by paintings by Jonathan Green.

"Where a Mirage Has Once Been, Life Must Be": The poem is inspired by the work of artist John Duckworth. The title is a line from John Ashbery's poem "Voyage in the Blue" from his book *Self-Portrait in a Convex Mirror*.

"The Weight It Takes": The poem was written for the inauguration of S.C. Governor Nikki Haley.

"February Triptych": The poem is dedicated to the memory of Kris Basala.

"Summer Dirge": The poem is dedicated to the memory of my step-father Robert Michael Tully.

"Brainstorming": The poem makes reference to Nikki Giovanni's poem "Knoxville, Tennessee."

"A Monstrous Terrible Story": The poem is inspired by Ellen Barry's article "Grim Village Shaken By Gruesome Mystery" (Lyovikha Journal), the *New York Times*, February 27, 2012.

"Rain Coming From a Bright Sky": Title is the caption for Photograph #34585 Nazi officers and female auxiliaries (Helferinnen) pose on a wooden bridge in Solahutte. July 1944, from Auschwitz through the lens of the SS: Photos of Nazi leadership at the camp. United States Holocaust Memorial Museum.

"Teen Wears Pet Bird Like a Hat," "Runaway Cow Tracked Down in Germany," and "Police Say Roving Cows Drank Backyard Brews": Poems are found poems inspired by newspaper wire service clippings.

"In My Light Year": The poem is inspired by a painting with same title by Rebecca Allan.

Poems in the first three sections are selected from three previous volumes: *Noticing Eden* (Hub City Writers Project, 2003); *Despite Gravity* (Ninety-Six Press, 2007); and *The Endless Repetition of an Ordinary Miracle* (Press 53, 2010).

Some of the poems, or different versions or sections of poems from the fourth section appeared in the following magazines: *Art Mag, Connotation Press: An Online Artifact, HEArt Online, Prairie Schooner, Reunion Journal, The Fledgling Rag,* and *Verb.*

Grateful acknowledgment is made to the editors of *An Endless Skyway, Poetry From the State Poets Laureate*. Edited by Caryn Mirrian-Goldberg, Marilyn L. Taylor, Denise Low and Walter Bargen. Ice Cube Books, North Liberty, Iowa, 2011, in which some of these poems first appeared.

Grateful acknowledgment goes to the Virginia Center for the Arts, where this manuscript was completed. Special thanks are owed to Jonathan Haupt, director of the University of South Carolina Press. Eternal thanks go to my husband, Peter, my first reader and editor, always.